Advance Praise for *A Small Rising Up in the Lungs*

"In *A Small Rising Up in the Lungs*, Kit Frick journeys, over land and sea, through silence and doubt, the destination always receding further into the distance. Always, in these poems, Frick's language is luminous and spare; here, danger shimmers beautifully just below the surface. 'In this place we define things,' Frick writes, 'in terms of absence,' and still these poems are insistent in their strength, in their presence."

— BRITTANY CAVALLARO
New York Times bestselling author
of the Charlotte Holmes series and *Girl-King*

"If the term *inspiration* denotes both creative invigoration and the intake of breath, then Kit Frick's poetry collection *A Small Rising Up in the Lungs* is a place where every line fills the reader with new fuel. In poems that feel at once contemporary and timeless, Frick teaches us to hold silence against our chest like a stunned wren, to place ourselves at the shore of real and imagined oceans, and to read passersby as a faint, familiar script. The poem 'Arroyo' instructs us that, 'In this place we define things. In terms of absence. No new / air. No saving grace. Our suspicion is: There are better ways / of understanding.' The pauses and absences in this collection grant us entry to the narrative, and allow us to breathe—and thrive—beneath its surface. This is a bright, mesmerizing debut, not to be missed."

— MARY BIDDINGER
author of *O Holy Insurgency* and *Small Enterprise*

"What's stunning about Kit Frick's *A Small Rising Up in the Lungs* is how she develops not only a sense of place, but a sense of people in that place—a place and people who exist both in the fantasy of imagined landscape and the settled quiet of the everyday. The language stuns, too; her fragments allow for multiple meaning; she builds for us an opening. She writes, 'our words can't contain the bigness of rooms,' but even more than bigness, Frick's words contain smallness—of the world, of the town, of the individual life. She brews a general sense of stasis, still but crushing, like the atmosphere on Venus. The book builds upon itself in layers that work like a pressure cooker, urging us to allow it to contain a little more, and a little more. Frick writes, 'I ask // a lot // adore me anyway.' She does, and I do."

— CAROLINE CABRERA
author of *Saint X* and *Flood Bloom*

"Kit Frick is a poet whose ear is tuned to the fine and particular. Her spare lines and muscular syntax build a troublesome dream of the American West that leaves us uneasily suspended between mystery and threat."

— REBECCA HAZELTON
author of *Fair Copy* and *Vow*

A SMALL RISING UP IN THE LUNGS

Other Titles by Kit Frick

FICTION

See All the Stars
(Simon & Schuster / Margaret K. McElderry Books, 2018)

POETRY

Echo, Echo, Light
(Slope Editions, 2013)

Kill Your Darlings, Clementine
(Rye House Press, 2013)

A SMALL RISING UP in the LUNGS

poems

Kit Frick

newamericanpress
Milwaukee, Wis.

new american press

© 2018 by Kit Frick

All rights reserved. No part of this publication may be reproduced, stored in a retrieval system, or transmitted, in any form or by any means, electronic, mechanical, photocopying, recording, or otherwise, without the prior written permission of the copyright holder.

Printed in the United States of America

ISBN 9781941561133

Interior design by Rob Carroll
Cover design by David Bowen

Cover image © Rachel B. Ostrow
https://www.rachelostrow.com/

For ordering information, please contact:
Ingram Book Group
One Ingram Blvd.
La Vergne, TN 37086
Phone: (800) 937-8000
Fax: (800) 876-0186
https://www.ingramcontent.com
orders@ingrambook.com

For event and media requests, please contact:
New American Press
www.newamericanpress.com
newamericanpress@gmail.com

CONTENTS

Kill Your Darlings, Clementine

13 [The men here sing]
14 [The men here are thick-lunged]
15 [The men have wives]
16 [The men here sing miner's songs]

Escape / Landscape

17 Arroyo
18 Escarpment
19 Avalanche Wind
20 Shoal
21 Bitter Lake
22 Bog

Kill Your Darlings, Clementine

23 [The men shave carefully]
24 [The men here hear things about God]
25 [The men here know]
26 [The men here know to kill]

Quarry

27 [each mark made white   imperfection]
28 [roadhouse steakout   whoop]
29 [twin lobsters at m/p]
30 [crickets   in my handprint]
31 [bout of happy]
32 [elemental mon]
33 [fashionable but not croquet   not]
34 [wild hooking thing   onto me]

Kill Your Darlings, Clementine

35 [The men have dreams]
36 [The men here see things at night]
37 [The men buy old cars only]
38 [The men make plans to revisit]
39 [The men here are underwater]

Escape / Landscape

40 Squall
41 Battery
42 Doldrums
43 Badlands
44 Nirvana
45 Breathing Cave

Kill Your Darlings, Clementine

46   [The men here want]
47   [The men have speaking parts]
48   [The men here are cruel]
49   [The men are in limbo]
50   [The men can't abide]
51   [The men here leave bags unattended]
52   [The men have begun their descent]

Quarry

53   [a fuller basket   metal]
54   [your steepled]
55   [net-cast & papaya-stuck]
56   [your hands globed   around lemons]
57   [a borrowed accord   fond]
58   [ruin too numerous]
59   [this cockamamie bulwark]
60   [all our accidents   tethered]

Kill Your Darlings, Clementine

61   [The men here are sick with urgency]
62   [The men here are buried alive]
63   [The men here wish to invent a new weather]
64   [The men here go swimming]
65   [The men here press ears to the wood grain]

After the Dig

66   After the Dig

Kill Your Darlings, Clementine

74   [The men here won't be]
75   [The men here repeat *new day*]
76   [The men here watch kites flown]
77   [The men here know how to be alive here]
78   [The men here see monsters]

79   Acknowledgments
83   About the Author

A SMALL RISING UP IN THE LUNGS

KILL YOUR DARLINGS, CLEMENTINE

::

The men here sing
only at night   sing loss

sing puncture
in the lungs   tar in the lungs

sing when no one listens
only   sing into bottles
then cork them

then release them   to the river

::

The men here are thick-lunged   small of air

they know the shortages of this place
how small becomes smaller   cough
turns choke

it is possible   if you will it
to breathe in unfriendly ratios

expel air abundantly   to take in so little
and live

::

The men have wives   or don't
have wives   either way

they are lonely   either way
they leave the sleepless bed alone

at night the men shuffle
feet across stone   across linoleum
across real hard wood

the language of shuffle   is known
to them only

the words that scuff
and then stop

::

The men here sing miner's songs
yet mine   for nothing

at night they inhabit flannel
and tan workmen's boots

to meet the wooded darkness
with love

unhoused   they let nothing
guide them

some nights   with bare hands
they dig holes in the ground

I will come back
tomorrow   I will bury something here

ESCAPE / LANDSCAPE

ARROYO

In this place we define things. In terms of absence. No new air. No saving grace. Our suspicion is: There are better ways of understanding. [Number them.] We watch the sky.

It doesn't rain for weeks. Instead of parched, say available. Not barren but open. There are people here who say they know the future. We know our future already. We say no thank you.

After days of heat, the clouds can bowl us over. We stagger. [We'd rather stagger.] We say we are filled already with molecules. [Thanks anyway.] We are humungous with sky.

ESCARPMENT

We didn't want to sail away—we wanted the whole ocean. We had salt on our lips. We wanted more and more of it. Because we couldn't have the ocean, we filled our stomachs and called ourselves satisfied.

We weren't satisfied. Walking along the concrete ridge between the cars and the shoreline, we couldn't hold the water in our sight. [The eyes are inadequate vessels.] We got discouraged, then resolved to be a different kind of alive. [Bird, child.]

At the end of the ridge, you put your hand in my hand. In our new life, you will be a grackle. I will be six. *Things could be so possible,* we said to each other. *From an aerial view. Or the helm of a boat.*

AVALANCHE WIND

Another way to think about [   ] is its inverse. There are better ways to cling to a dead thing. Fists are weak. Try a headlock. Try each floorboard until one gives way. Take a long drive through six mountains and feel the dead drilling through stone. Don't think about collapsible wingspan. Breakable objects. The possible life span of a trumpeter swan. So many cars traveling through [the space that stone left]. Another way to think about [   ] is what can it hold. Press the backs of your hands against the doorframe until your arms float up like wings [^ ^]. This is what weightless feels like. Resurrection or something close.

SHOAL

This is the meat of it. Pink or unpink. Rare or breathing [still]. In how many ways can we compare what makes us up to what we love. Cedar : sailboat :: flesh : animal. [We go on trying.] The sway of my back collects what the sky gives away free. Number the drops until a pool forms. I am face-pressed to the ground. A pool forms. Shallow : water :: shallow : breath. There are many ways to signal danger. Someone erects a sign by my side. *Please clear the area. Can be hazardous to boating.*

BITTER LAKE

I could talk about the smell but. I'd rather listen to gulls. How their cry can be haunting in flight [searchers] it carries with you. I've read birds can see beyond the visible spectrum [human spectrum]. I sit on the hood of a parked car. I sit like I'm in yoga, like I could sit like this all day. No one compliments my posture or yells *hey get off my car*.

There are magnetic fields hidden in plain sight. I try to sense one.

If the light off this bitter lake is ultraviolet. If the eye could be a window to anywhere.

BOG

It was February and everything tinted green around the edges. [Like new growth or sea glass, but sadder.] I was wearing my sadglasses. I couldn't take them off. I was filled with bitter melon and river water. I couldn't spit it out. Everybody had an opinion. I was better off, what didn't kill me, etc. and so forth. I didn't listen. I opened my closet of miracle cures. Some were shaped like paper birds and some were heavy as oil tankers in the night.

[Nothing   worked.]

Without you, it was hard to see myself clearly. The mirror was tinted green around the edges. *Gone* was so finite and impossible to swallow. [Like sadness or shattered glass.] Your absence sat like a dead thing on my tongue. I wanted to leave on a tanker in the night. I wanted nothing clearly.

KILL YOUR DARLINGS, CLEMENTINE

::

The men shave carefully   or forget
to shave   the mirror's contents stay stubborn

it doesn't trouble them   why go looking
go instead into the yard

problems out here are simple
to identify   easily resolved

weeds in the garden   pollen coats the car
the men take the wheel

they whistle low and minor   they talk back
to crows

::

The men here hear things about God
mercy's handiwork   what is unknowable
what is grace

they feel diminished by it   obscured
        unable to sort

salt water from the sea   water from salt

the bigness of words rendered
nothing at all   in this place

their bodies rendered no one
becoming only casing   and strung
from a clothes line
flappable

in all directions   all imagined meanings

::

The men here know
where gold is   where oil

they leave it alone

know it's best not to dig
too much

best not to uncover   veins
in other bearings

::

The men here know to kill
your darlings   to kill your daughters
    with blindness   is the only way

to let them leave this place

the men practice breathing
into paper bags
practice unsightedness   unsoundedness

they leave no mark

practice speaking into the back of a hand

QUARRY

*

each mark made white   imperfection

engine

      a tiny storm   hibernal

*

seam or unseam

wash or

*

roadhouse steakout   whoop

it up   flex vim

& vigor

        holler

*

this little bovine cried wee-wee-wee-

wee

*

twin lobsters at m/p

two tines   burnished

    little bits

*

    pick steel

paper covers rock

*

crickets   in my handprint

full yellow noise   sing it,

Saturday

*

a great fondness   or

bravery

*

bout of happy

we tumbler clink   speak

        easy these days

*

days of bitters   say

starfish

*

    elemental mon

    sturgeon   as champagne bursts

    fancy against lips   bliss

*

        brotherhood

    of roe   salt kin

*

fashionable but not croquet   not

the parlor   this vestigial

estate

*

warning signs   mind

the curios

*

wild hooking thing   onto me

onto any aching reason

      latch

*

feral hands   make

wild work

KILL YOUR DARLINGS, CLEMENTINE

::

The men have dreams   they do
wild dreams   waking dreams

of boats mostly   endless
ocean

but not California
Mexico

The Cape of Good Hope

their ocean is frozen
Arctic   they bring axes

release fish
trapped beneath ice

::

The men here see things at night
birds tracing the sky

ice shooting up brick

a small face in an upstairs window
then curtained   then darkened
then gone

above   and along the ground
a lessening of color

the men don't see   a win
in daybreak

                no swift departure
nothing broken   away from

::

The men buy old cars only
the kind equipped   with manual-op windows
those sturdy physical cranks

they prepare for disaster   the unlikely event
of a water landing

in case   of complete submersion

the men know how   to avoid
drowning

they practice swimming in the bathtub at night

::

The men make plans to revisit
someone else's childhood

a string of years   unhindered by memory
      a borrowed past

they manufacture nostalgia
on envelope backs   old directions to route 51
grocery slips

weeks later   the men squint close
to decipher their fabrications

these are my V's   *this should make sense*

::

The men here are underwater   no gear
no gills

flesh against salt
the muscled liquid pressing

they come up for air when they must
just like anyone   but above water feels

a hell of a lot like under
the way grains of sugar parrot   grains of salt
in the dish

the way we reduce
to mimicry   the rationed air

storm's coming   dark and close

impossible to see your feet clearly
no sight   of land

ESCAPE / LANDSCAPE

SQUALL

I start to organize, but nothing matches. We delay our trip, and then we delay again. I ask if you're angry with me. [What I did in your dream.] I can't stop checking the weather. You say no, but I wonder. How these items should go with these items, but the drawer won't hold it all. How this used to be a complete set. We say we should get on the road by six. We look at the sky, we look at our phones. We try to gauge the proper level of threat.

We fill the tires. Your eyes follow me across the air stream. [What I did in your dream.] How "miscellany" is the anti-label. We get on the road by eight. We agree we know the drive so well. The dark won't hold us back.

BATTERY

It is possible for hands to float like water lilies. [August, poolside.] There are women here who fan themselves for hours. I'd rather greet the sun. What is this talk of foundation. Stable or unstable. Bolted or anchors aweigh. I am belly-pressed to the concrete edge. I place my palms on the surface. This talk of departure. Someone's father is a father again in Nevada. Someone refuses to miss him. It's possible for hands to float away if you let them. Some have made it to the ocean. [If you swallow the gossip.] Some find enduring calm.

DOLDRUMS

Night comes in a slow bloom of abandon. Our words can't contain the bigness of rooms. Our rooms hold failure nicely. I didn't ask for this. [We ask for so little of what makes us up.] Remember the coffee table was always dirty. The days ended in a sloe gin fizz. I was never afraid, except of your death, which would come one day thieving. How can I hold my hands in a perfect cup? I squeeze the sides together until it burns. Could I hold water? Could I rupture? We've been here before. We know this juncture. The photograph of you swinging a glass door wide. The evening ushered in. The slow bloom of voices carried up from the street, and no answers to the pressing questions, the ones that could carry the story forward.

BADLANDS

Prior attempts to typify rely heavily on absence. We read the reports and get stoned. A lack of feature can be defining, and yet. Say eroded. To bone. Taste the roof of your mouth. The two tongue taps, the rich red clay. There's chalk in our blood. In the soil, coal seams. Fossil rock. Outlaws in the valley town. We get down with our badness. [Difficult to navigate. Difficult to love.] Barefoot and boozed-up, we kiss bottles then pitch them. We know the future. The dark of the ravine. The whistle, the smash. In the nothing that follows, we flex our badness. It fills us with heat. We could let it define us. We could let the desert.

NIRVANA

If you change charged particles into radiant beams, does it mean god? If you go to a party at the Soho Grand. If you wear your mother's wedding dress. When I get there, there will be right things to say. [Learned things. Like thank you.] There will be maps transposed on maps transposed on maps. This one plots for stoplights. This one plots for lost things. Don't be afraid of confusion. [Confusion is a permanent state.] There is an art to being gracious. [Say bless your heart.] Everybody do the collision course. Everybody super collide.

BREATHING CAVE

I come here when: The bridge to nowhere reinvents itself [resurrects] as a dam. I need to feel the air in both directions. I want to say it passes through me, but really: It's like water punching rock, full of threat, then gone. Like urgency then what remains. [It echoes.] As in respiration. As in river and more river. I come here when I need the breathing to overcome me. If breath denotes life, then this mountain. It's all I want to think about. These airstreams. This massive lung.

KILL YOUR DARLINGS, CLEMENTINE

::

The men here want   in a way
inscrutable   to themselves

to those who wish
to ask   but don't

they smoke because their lungs ache
for the dead air   they pity it
home it   swaddle it

there is less to say

::

The men have speaking parts   on Wednesdays
only   know the language on Thursdays

the other days are blurred
to the background   extras in their own lives

they want more sound   kick tires
until their boots ring   pierce bullets

through soda cans in the backyard   they pop
like hot grease in the air

the men here feel empty
still   feel the softness of their bodies

the crush of no noise   after the gun's
been put down

::

The men here are cruel   by some estimations
withholders of gesture
embrace

it's very personal   but not how you think
this is infection's way

they keep
a prudent distance   they spare you

have learned things
about mercy

::

The men are in limbo
always   always between this and that

the afternoon's longness   night's blind

suitcases packed always   always the task
of rifling for a toothbrush   a work shirt
a belt

why   can't I dig
in my heels

why won't this stick

::

The men can't abide   the laws
of this place

the sequential order   held fast

some voices are weaker than others
some operate   in different registers

the men hum in the frenetic way
a phone hums when called   they say aloud

I am a vessel   a phone   or no
a refrigerator

::

The men here leave bags unattended
then wear a mustache and glasses   then watch

from the water fountain   to see what happens
nothing ever happens

a man with a badge walks by and keeps walking

this deviance used to be fun   now the stakes
are terrible

no one laughs   or notices either

::

The men have begun their descent
through cloud   feel hollowed

by it   rocked by it   whited out

how difficult to maintain   pressure found
at sea level

the chambers of the brain   switching off
one by one   shutting down

the chambers of sinew   chambers
of bone

how simple to feel elevated one day   aloft
buoyed up   then

dropped then   brakeless   then

nothing but weight

QUARRY

*

a fuller basket   metal,

moral   bags of sand

cry ballast

*

unclasp everything   going,

going, gone

*

your steepled

      hands   fingers

all in tandem

Sunday pop-up shop

*

holy getup

      shine &

squeak

*

net-cast & papaya-stuck

any little floss   clichéd

today   any cheat

*

not seamless

anything   but easy

*

your hands globed   around lemons

rarefied yellow   sour

glories today

*

later, limousines

roll by slow

*

a borrowed accord   fond

      of some likeness

some recherché thing

*

everything hinges   seems

to hinge

*

ruin too numerous

no hard math   no factory tour

      mount

*

      an apology

this megaphone audibly

*

this cockamamie bulwark

    sea foam & string

let's laugh about

*

after the rupture   after

laughter

*

all our accidents   tethered

all our resplendent selves

    I ask

*

    a lot

adore me anyway

KILL YOUR DARLINGS, CLEMENTINE

::

The men here are sick with urgency   and nowhere
to place it   their hands are ready   so ready

where is their burden   where is the thing
that needs fixing

they pace until no inch of floor
remains untrodden   no unruffled carpet

*if this is a test of my patience   you win
don't you hear me calling* uncle

this is the longest day   *uncle*
    each hour is the longest

::

The men here are buried alive
by their own doing   own hands

they know it   come to terms
yes   I am ready to reach now

*let my hands do the work   the hard
work of reaching*

let me extend them out   to what

::

The men here wish to invent a new weather

spend hours locked in laboratories   a test tube
of smog   winter stoppered in glass

what is mixed already must be unmixed   distilled
to genesis   *if I can take*

all this sunshine   all this thick fog
if I can sort out each element   remix it

what we need is unexpected   a pink party cake
some cause for celebration

::

The men here go swimming
in the neighbor's pool   without asking

it's night   the floodlights
make the water big and special

the men feel undone   by all the brightness
though no one sees   everyone sleeps

the men go under   where there's less light

as a kid I could hold my breath
two minutes twelve seconds

::

The men here press ears to the wood grain   listen
for its breath

what can objects tell us   of life and death
rebirth   about a living past

before becoming machined things

the men want answers   not the same hollow
offerings   feel themselves turning

toward elsewhere

AFTER THE DIG

After the dig, we feel the earth acutely. Our arms reverberate. We twang for days. At night, we dream we are still digging. We wake exhausted. We've been shoveling the dark, and the stars weigh a ton. In the mornings, our muscles knot in sympathy with our dreams. We drag ourselves to the shower. We find dirt in our teeth.

I'm sorry I missed you, I was searching. I was part of the party. We had flashlights and helicopter coverage. We used our best radio voices. When we found her, there were hugs and cake but also there was so much time. The day emptied out in front of me. My hands needed a flashlight or a GPS device. My throat wanted a name to call out. That night, I went back, I was searching. I needed a mission, something to find. I was in the woods, and I let in the dark. I felt it burrow into my skin. I took it with me. I took it home.

After the ocean, we feel the land travel through us. Something was stoppered, and then unstoppered. We throw a dock party. We eat watermelon and fresh berries. Someone gets a seahorse tattoo. Someone blasts "Born in the U.S.A." We feel drunk on our land legs. When we dance, it feels like we've never moved before. Later, the earth realigns and loses its strangeness. We feel a little empty. If we're honest, we feel a little thankful.

I'm sorry I missed you, time lost track of me. I was sitting on the train. I had lives and then more lives. Today was a window and I saw straight through it. Tomorrow would come, and I could just sit still. Time ran above me and beside me but also through me, and I had it all figured it out. I don't feel this way often. You know I'm always searching. My head lamp on. Boots to the ground. I'll make things right tomorrow. It felt so good to stop.

After the phone call, we don't know how to fix things. We offer solutions anyway. We throw them on the table and let them grow cold. We can't look our failures in the eye. We feel useless and then we feel worse about it. We hold hands and feel a little comfort. We say we'll go out for a drive. We'll pick up ice cream. We'll make an airship from this lead balloon.

I'm sorry I was late, I was at the river. I was listening to no one. I was making time. How long before bottle glass becomes beautiful? I am gathering water and salt. I am asking my questions into this wet, rushing thing. Don't they call it a confluence, when rivers meet? What about saliva? What about blood?

After the rain, we feel a little better. But I wouldn't say clean. I wouldn't go that far. What we feel is a small rising up in the lungs. A minor adjustment. Like there are possibilities, and we might have our pick. Like something is coming, and it's good, and we'll hold it and press it to our chests and feel some wonder there.

A SMALL RISING UP IN THE LUNGS

I'm sorry I was late, I was on the highway. I was counting exit signs and trying to add them up to something to tell you. There are so many ways off the highway. People live there. We don't, and I don't know how I feel about that. I think I feel a little cheated. I want to knock on all those doors and look inside. This one has a big bay window. This one has a turret. All those houses, and we're not there. Let's go there. All those garden plots. All those backyards rolling down to rivers.

KILL YOUR DARLINGS, CLEMENTINE

::

The men here won't be   forever   some won't
some see salvation in a car door   a plan

follow these three steps   they lead you to the highway
the men drive with precision   each mirror checked

a clemency granted   for each past wrong
their hands feel no less dirty   no less harmed
       let it pass

but not in this place   not when gravity
not the river

::

The men here repeat *new day*
new day new day　beneath breath

the rolling hills　　　the carbonous dark
of Pennsylvania　　　the question remains

how to fill these panels
of time　which remains unbankable

why can't I save it　for a better state

the strong suspicion is　　a new weather
won't be enough　　　not a whole factory
of weather

it's best to start with some simple thing
a slice of pear　　　a pair
of socks　　　　　then wait

for something to lift

::

The men here watch kites flown   at staggering
angles   each competes with the sunset

I am the deepest red   I contain God

the men sip tea from thermoses   or hot soup
they think   *I will wait a while*   *I will sit*

with the sky
it deepens quickly in this place   it bolds
without regret

what will the sky hold   when I go
I will hold this   fiercely

::

The men here know how to be alive here
when asked they will say   it's the one useful thing

I have learned in this place   it's the one thing I will carry
on my back   when I go

if I ever go   and what of your wives
we will ask   and what of your daughters

they will go ahead   the men say
I have taught them how not to know me

they will look ahead
only   they will unvex their own pass

::

The men here see monsters   in the cloudmass
like children   like anyone

today I will admit to looking

this is a fang   this is a mess
of claws

through the windshield   the monsters darken
the country sky

this is a warning   you'd better look
and stay looking

no this is an offering   *I will call it*
what it is   new wild blue

this is a pioneering sky   this is an unveiling

ACKNOWLEDGMENTS

This collection has been a long time in the making, and while writing is a mostly solitary endeavor, these poems were hardly created in a vacuum. I owe deep gratitude to the undergraduate creative writing program at Sarah Lawrence College, particularly to Kate Knapp Johnson, Jeffrey McDaniel, Mark Wunderlich, David Hollander, and the brilliant students with whom I studied, who took my writing seriously even in its most vernal and sometimes cringe-worthy stages, and encouraged me to pursue a creative life. Equal gratitude is owed to the MFA program at Syracuse University, particularly to my brilliant cohort; my insightful thesis advisor Bruce Smith; faculty Michael Burkard, Arthur Flowers, Brooks Haxton, Mary Karr, Christopher Kennedy, Dana Spiotta, and George Saunders; and staff Sarah Harwell and Terri Zollo, with whom I spent three intense years immersed in poetry and prose, learning to become more fully and vividly alive.

Thank you also to my ever-supportive parents, Pat and Tony, and my loving husband and number one fan, Osvaldo, who give me the courage and encouragement to put writing first.

Enormous thanks to my editor at New American Press, David Bowen, and to 2017 New American Poetry Prize judge Jesse Lee Kercheval for selecting *A Small Rising Up in the Lungs* for publication and ushering it into the world. Thank you to the inimitable Rachel Ostrow for allowing us to use her gorgeous work on the book's cover and to Rob Carroll for designing the book's interior. Thank you to the MacDowell Colony, the Constance Saltonstall Foundation for the Arts, and the Kimmel Harding Nelson Center for the Arts for finding value in these poems and offering me time and space to work. Thank you also to the editors at The National Poetry Series, Colorado State University's Center for Literary Publishing, the University of Akron Press, Big Lucks Books, the Cleveland State University Poetry Center, Subito Press, and Omnidawn for recognizing and encouraging earlier versions of this manuscript.

Finally, my sincere thanks to the editors of the publications in which these poems first appeared, sometimes in earlier forms, or with different titles:

Anti-: "[The men have dreams]" and "[The men here see things at night]"
Better: "[The men here are cruel]," "[The men can't abide]," and "[The men have begun their descent]"
Bone Bouquet: "[The men here sing miner's songs]" and "[The men shave carefully]"
Brightly Press, *Shake the Tree* anthology (2015): "[net-cast & papaya-stuck]," "[fashionable but not croquet   not]," "[elemental mon]," "[bout of happy]," "[your steepled]," "[wild hooking thing   onto me]," "[a borrowed accord   fond]," and "[ruin too numerous]"
Brooklyn Poets Anthology (2017): "Avalanche Wind"

Crazyhorse: "Arroyo" (reprinted on *Verse Daily*) and "Avalanche Wind"
Failbetter: "After the Dig"
Forklift, Ohio: "[The men here repeat *new day*]" and "[The men here watch kites flown]"
Ghost Town: "Bitter Lake," "Battery," and "Bog"
Hobart: "Doldrums," "Badlands," "Nirvana," and "Breathing Cave"
interrupture: ["The men make plans to revisit"] and ["The men here are underwater"]
Likewise Folio: "[each mark made white   imperfection]," "[a fuller basket   metal]," "[roadhouse steakout   whoop]," and "[crickets in my handprint]"
New Delta Review: "[The men here want]," "[The men here know]," "[The men here know to kill]," "[The men are in limbo]," and "[The men here leave bags unattended]"
OmniVerse: "[The men here are sick with urgency]"
Poor Claudia / Phenome: "[your steepled]," "[twin lobsters at m/p]," and "[net-cast & papaya-stuck]"
Prick of the Spindle: "[your hands globed around lemons]," "[this cockamamie bulwark]," and "[all our accidents   tethered]"
Sixth Finch: "[The men here sing]"
Thrush Press, *Broadside Series #24*: "[The men here wish to invent a new weather]"

Some of the poems in this manuscript also appeared in the limited-edition chapbook *Kill Your Darlings, Clementine* (Rye House Press, 2013).

KIT FRICK is a novelist, poet, and MacDowell Colony fellow. Originally from Pittsburgh, PA, she studied creative writing at Sarah Lawrence College and received her MFA from Syracuse University. When she isn't putting complicated characters in impossible situations, Kit edits poetry and literary fiction for a small press, edits for private clients, and mentors emerging writers through Pitch Wars. Her debut young adult novel is *See All the Stars* (Simon & Schuster / Margaret K. McElderry Books, 2018). *A Small Rising Up in the Lungs* is her debut poetry collection.

www.ingramcontent.com/pod-product-compliance
Lightning Source LLC
LaVergne TN
LVHW041345080426
835512LV00006B/611